Once in a while, a poetry book comes along and startles the human conscience and imagination and inspires a generation of people to debate its importance to literature and to the commonweal of nations.
This is such a book.

The author's writing tugs at our sensibility as we stroll along with him in our living embodiment of life.

We would be wise to respond to this work as added worth to our perception of who we are as a universal race of people.

What a wonderful gift we have received!

Providential Realities Press
Memphis
2023

Awakened *as the* Impossible Dream

Uncommon Poetry

JOE HANKINS III

Awakened as the Impossible Dream

For information about this title or to order other books and/or electronic media, contact the publisher:

Providential Realities Press
prpress.edu@aol.com

ISBNs:
979-8-9860134-0-4 (hardcover)
979-8-9860134-1-1 (softcover)
979-8-9860134-2-8 (eBook)

Printed in the United States of America

Cover and Interior design: 1106 Design

To

the unknown faces who silently weep,

may your journey be rewarded.

Coming soon:
(title subject to change)

Imagine God
Communicating with an Agitated Soul

Awakened as the Impossible Dream is poetry at its finest, written from divine illumination. In the first chapter, God burnishes a wayward man's heart, reveals Joseph's true identity, and ordains him to be His trumpet.

[This extensive, dramatic poem has begged to be fully exposed and to have its message impressed in the mind of this land. Consequently, in another book to be published later, I have enlarged upon this message; thus, a play is born.]

Awakened as the Impossible Dream also presents poems carved out of human affairs and emotions destined, along with the intricate poem in the first chapter, to be a meaningful looking glass for everyday people.

Contents

Acknowledgments

I am eternally grateful to my mother, Geraldine, for always being a peaceful, thoughtful lady and an enlightened Christian.

Thanks to my father, Joseph; sisters Mattie, Mary, Marilyn, Madeleine, Sandra, and Georgetta; brothers Joel, Jarvis, and Edward; and to my spiritually blood brother, Jerry Jeffries. Their trust, including my mom, in a dreamer stabilizes me when darkness taints my path.

Pat Taylor, my first angel: I can never thank her enough. She enthusiastically believes in me and in my work and has typed and proofread most of my writings. She is endearing to me, and I salute her. Salute!

Frida Medini: may the angels make room in their domain for Frida because she has become one of them. She blew the dust off my eyes, and I saw the stars. Frida is a kind and gentle woman, yet she pushed me toward my destiny.

Sylvia Carruth: a wonderful lady who I admire for her wisdom and beauty and grace. Perhaps without her realizing so, I trust her opinions regarding my writing.

I send my love and peace to Anna. Denise, you are loved.

Much thanks to Christopher Robbins, proofreader; April Jones, editor; Katherine Riegel, proofreader. A special thanks to Jeanette Flowers, my longtime and forever spiritual comrade.

Many thanks to the tender souls who have shared space and time with me. I owe each of you much.

I thank God for everything.

A Piece of Heaven

A Piece of Heaven

I

Angel

Lightning fractured a jawbone.
Layers of coated smut
greeted the blundering creature
umpteen ages ago.

The man,
worn to a frazzle,
reaped the indignation
of a folly.

Heaven
frizzled away.
An untenable voice
folded his mouth.

Like an unwound spool of thread,
like sifted fine flour,
like gum pasted on a doorbell,
he was unearthed, pulverized, deserted.

He cast his bread
upon the water.
Much blood was sacrificed,
an assassination was prolonged.

Antique hope yet simmered
though darkness besieged his heart.
His mind's eye formed an image,
the smoldered image smiled.

A marriage proposal evolved,
the man and the surging image
sighted a path to elope.
Together, they faced the redemptive, cosmic journey.

Brutal men,
cunning dames,
a raggedy, renegade heart
could not deface their rendezvous with destiny.

II

God

O wayward child,
who nursed you?
Whose sucking Breasts
staved off starvation?

Little boy, little boy,
who cried for you?
Whose Teardrops
fought the savages feasting on your flesh?

Earth child, earth child,
who entered into your tomb?
Whose Lungs propped you up
made death behave?

Joseph

O Sage,
O my soul,
lips tightened,
understanding's void.

Cantatrice,
my nose runs,
eyes sweat,
what song will you sing?

Singer

The song is unsingable,
the words cannot be spoken.
It is forbidden
to disrupt the branding of a flea.

III

Joseph

My rod is broken,
I cannot strive,
yet I hear
footsteps marching onward.

IV

Joseph

I am skating!
I am skating on water:
two swollen knees, two swollen elbows,
my life preserver is being tested.

God

When will you learn?
How long, how long My conceived child
must I fasten your trousers?
Stand up; see the Light.

V

Angel

A gauging Light
breaks the reign of idiocy.
Reason is seen crawling injuriously,
sniffing the cankerous dust.

God

Look! Look! Look at the divine reflection
reverberating off the Mirror!
It is a sign
of who you are!

Please! Look once more,
look inside your cramped compartment,
a self is immobilized,
he screams for you!

Joseph

Oh my,
that's a strange person.
Definitely, he is an alien,
I know him not.

God

Joseph,
a religious rift
sawed asunder a soul.
Go and meet yourself.

Inhale.
Breathe in the inspiration, revelation;
digest the manna,
you are My offspring.

It is I,
your asexual Parent:
your Mother, your Father,
I love you.

It is I,
you have dishonored Me,
cast shame upon My Crown,
I love you.

It is I,
your soul senses My Presence.
Men, women: they spear you,
I love you.

You have wandered far away,
abandoned your divine self,
seemed alienated from grace,
I have come for you.

Joseph

I am abased,
confusion coughs about me.
This town, this capsized molehill,
I have joined it. I am a citizen in ruins.

God

You are unnatural; mad.
That serpent's town cannot substitute
the Royal Palace, your Birthplace.
Think. I have given you wisdom.

Joseph

My wisdom is spilled,
secreted on the ground.
I cannot think,
bruises are on my forehead.

Indeed, I have drifted far away.
Every night, a chilled basement,
a smoking furnace, thumping pipes,
a rattling hot water tank await me.

Whose son am I,
I cannot tell:
Earth, Heaven: the streets are barren,
Your Light must bear me.

Walk with me!
Walk in my footsteps!
Walk in the hellfire!
I am burning!

God

Joseph, stand boldly,
stand in the Peak of the Day,
stand in the Resurrected Light,
stand in the Most Holy Place.

Be inspired, be transformed,
be exalted. Be!
I love you.
Love, now, your most holy self.

Behold the Light:
It is My Eye, My Spirit,
your Lover, your Redeemer;
It is the Womb that birthed you!

Joseph

My Mother, my Father,
my Lover, my God,
I have sinned.
I am corrupted. I am dust.

God

You are My son,
image of My Being,
breath of My Life,
love of My Heart.

Hush, hush,
"Peace, be still."
The sun shines this day,
its approval is etched on your face.

Go to the Crystalline Brook,
drink heartily,
drink the Wine of Life,
live as you once have lived.

See proudly
your noble self,
O prince of God.
Visit the King.

Go hastily
My dear son.
Hurry, hurry Home!
The porter is at the Door.

Leave your scarlet robe behind,
drag it no farther.
Your royal apparel is laundry,
it will be given to you.

Joseph

How can I distrust You,
You speak artfully.
You are the Guiding Compass,
I will follow You.

I shall shed
my scarlet robe.
Pell-mell fever draped me
the moment it touched my heart.

Death perspired on my pillows,
nagging, howling for attention.
His plea amplified; grew crazy,
often pillows were replaced.

In Death's arms,
Father, I cried to Thee:
freedom, O freedom.
Freedom was but a myth.

I hid,
Death found me, abused me.
My life is his death,
his death is my life.

I'll go!
Yes! Take me Home,
only be tender conscience,
for I am wounded.

God

Freedom is here.
Open your tainted heart.
Freedom will envelop then permeate your passion,
your aspiration. Receive it; rejoice in it.

Reason with Me.
All there is, is Mine,
what is not, is Mine.
I AM ALL THERE IS.

I AM your conscience.
You live because
I AM Alive
feeding you Life.

Life I give you,
love is your freedom,
the sweat on your pillows,
It is I, loving you.

Joseph

Speechless.
How can I speak.
In love is no death,
life is forever.

VI

Angel

On the roof
of a screened-in chicken coop,
an alert rooster crows.
Dawn has come.

On the pinnacle of the Temple
in the Holy City, Jerusalem,
a thoroughbred prince, the prodigal son,
regains his balance.

Heaven hums to him:
welcome Home,
saddle up,
you are at your beginning.

God

Prepare to march:
the beggar on the left,
the aristocrat on the right,
they are your shadows.

Split not,
march erectly,
arm not a sword,
salvation rides with you.

Trot to the haughty mainland,
notice the bloody emblems and embroideries
resting on tycoons' shoulders,
toast quickly and leave.

Gallop to the gleaning peninsula,
notice the hibernating ants,
visit the ailing creatures,
pray quickly and leave.

Scramble to the wretched byway,
notice the weary proselytes,
look into the sinners' eyes,
teach quickly and leave.

Race to the dwindling hinterland,
notice the approaching wagon train,
dismount and study the peasants,
learn quickly and leave.

Aim for the wanton highway,
wear seeless[1] sunglasses,
sealed earplugs,
do not stop!

Hurdle over booby traps,
skip not a stride,
entertain no thoughts,
run on!

Point upward and look below:
bridges, roads, ships, ferryboats,
where are they going—
to the ends of the worlds.

Hell enlarges itself,
earth grumbles,
mountains quiver,
mice are in a frenzy.

No one understands the season.
It is here!
Judgment Day is here.
Human carnage is being buried.

---

1 I created seeless from the word sightless. The tone of it feels right and worthy for this verse.

Joseph,
you are My trumpet.
Sound the alarm,
awake the cities.

Gather My chosen people
lest they faint.
Go again, my son,
go back, face the toothless beast.

The Finger of God
is thy Pillar.
You are ready, brazenly fortified.
Go and do My Bidding.

You are yoked to Me,
bonded to the Eternal Light.
I am your Shield.
Go and sit upon Earth's throne.

Tell them who steal,
it is not too late.
Tell them who kill,
it is not too late.

Tell them who hate,
it is not too late.
Tell them who seek Me not,
I AM GLORIFIED IN MY PEOPLE.

Tell the hypocrites,
preach no more,
sit down.
Their words are idle.

Heaven is not closed,
false voices must be silenced,
no one speaks for Me,
only My son and his staff.

Joseph

This burden is great,
the world is crazy,
humans masquerade as gods and goddesses;
it is appointed, they must be silenced.

I'll go into the belly of hell.
I will go
in the Spirit
of my Father.

The name Joseph is too trivial,
too inadequate,
too imperfect,
too unjust.

My Father,
give me a new Name,
a Royal Name for identification,
a Name for life.

God

A new Name!
Take My Name with you,
it is enough,
use it discreetly.

Joseph

The prince's robe, please!
I am earthbound,
my loin must be indomitable,
the earthlings are ruffled.

VII

Angel

The squirrel cage is bound,
eyes are fuzzy,
coup de grace is not ordered.
The New Age waves joyously.

Praise God!

A Touch of Love

No More Dreams to Dream

My pen lies at your door,
seems it has run out of ink.
Miles of thoughts,
years of shedding sweat,
answered and unanswered dreams,
they have instantaneously evaporated.

The Running River

It came to be.
No other force churned so freely,
rested so easily.

Long-winded droughts,
slow-driven mystiques
could not hamper nature's engagement.

The running river's distant legs
hosted heaven's uttered promise.
It came to be.

A Time to Be

Two realities merging by dreams adrift;
thoughts, numb and aloft, await
until the next moment becomes this moment
in a time meant to be.

White Shadow

Two years, two quivering years
a shadow sat in my imagination,
pounding on the breath I breathed
until, at last, I stopped breathing;
I saw a white swan dancing in the air—
a beautiful sight to behold.
She noticed not my dutiful appearance,
not my fanciful, belabored countenance
choking on its final hope stirring—
my face, lost in a maze of self-intentions.
The angelic swan twirled out of a shadow,
turned into a snowflake,
melted in my hand.
Her face saw mine.

The Muse in Eternity

Written in the soul of eternality
even before the universe's eye contained visualization
of two illuminating beings coming—
a mystique man and an eloquent woman—
"a piece of history's future turned to the distant past,
faced the arrival of a heartfelt rejuvenation,
honored the Muse's sacred oath."
They stepped onto the stage unscripted,
about them, books had spoken:
"In timeless poems and in wasted time living,
in deferred promises and in dreams kept alive,
in ceaseless heartaches toiling in lumps of clay,
in a spontaneous heap of joy and in an empty
  bed humming,
a necessary providential happening occurred."

Not Gone

She waited
he'd lost much—
his mother, his wife,
his God, his identity,
gone

yet she waited
he stared at a contentious avalanche—
an unabated streaming mischief
corralling and stalling his advancements,
he saw a vagabond mirroring him

but she waited
he'd lost a jewel—
his greatest belief and love;
she once trusted him too,
he knew sorrow

still she waited
a gentle lamb,
a love that wouldn't leave,
a heart that fought tears,
not gone

Let's Dream Together

come by and sit
let's dream together
as hurt drifts away
we'll find new life

why not stay awhile
find lost pearls hidden
somewhere here between
you and me

it's impossible to lose
fate's brought us reality
we'll sit together here
as from out of a tale

come by and sit
we're not constrained
rich is our desire
can't contain it anymore

why not stay awhile
we have the answer
to each other's heart
it's impossible to lose

come by and sit
why not stay awhile
let's dream together
it's impossible to lose

it's impossible to lose
wise is our choice
rich is our desire
can't contain it anymore

A Day like Today

A day like today
stars humming a new melody
I'm trying to figure out what to say—
I think I'll start over once more

For you, I battle to write
in the comfort of chosen words
to free you from sorrow and hurt
uproot thistles, plant new life

See beyond yesterday's storm
dew is on the morning soil
calm's baked in today
walk in water, wiggle your toes

You come a long way
to find another dream
what is life without delights
head to the mountains for a night

Good morning stars are singing
all around flowers blooming
fluff your pillow, say hello
to a day like today

Loving Bigfoot

Freely, Frida dances with Bigfoot—
I'm here and there, visible and invisible,
undivided by space and distance,
always, quickly leaping out of the day,
fleeting into the night.
But, somehow, she sees my impressionable image,
she paints me, kisses me, squeezes me,
puts her love onto my face.
She's a fascinating, ingenious queen
floating away from her quiet palace,
playing and resting on my playground, the cloud—
a boundless zone of imaginative satisfaction.
I am Bigfoot, a gigantic notion,
she feels the mystery of my being
perching in an ancient stratosphere.
Her urges and loneliness blanket my invisibleness,
her quest has found me, Bigfoot.

A Touch of Love

Loan me the heel of a kiss,
not the rich chocolate kind
or the vanilla cream
melting.

Loan me your cheeks,
a puff of weightless heights,
two climbable mountains—
a touch of love.

Loan me worth,
all of who you are,
to my broken sanctuary.
Loan me your crown!

Ride in my chariot!
Ride with me!
Ride to my naval base
stationed somewhere in my sight!

Plant a necessary kiss
under the lid of my swollen eye.
Fertilize my sweat
with your tears.

Plant rubies and diamonds,
all of your sensation,
into my awareness.
Let me see you naked.

Sweet Love

Like an open water hydrant,
Frida's love pours out,
racing to celebrate her feelings.

Like the singing of dawn,
a newborn baby,
all the stars in the galaxies,

like a fresh thought smiling,
a drop of rain on a leaf,
a symphony orchestra playing in a forest,

like midnight's silence,
Frida delicately inhales and exhales life.
Naturally, openly, daringly she loves.

A Rose for Frida

Inside a gift package,
inside you,
inside the yearn,
inside sweetness,

inside a living beat
beating as your soul
lies an immortal self
looking at me.

I see you swimming in a thousand dimensions
even across long distant waters.
In running creeks, in picturesque waterfalls
even in sacred moving moments,

I see your heart always loving.
You are a beanstalk
spreading upwardly,
higher and higher—

the higher you go,
you see yourself
watching Earth,
you see me watching you.

A gift you are—
you living ev'ry beat and second,
planting all of you
into now's nuances.

Measure the esteem's worth of love,
measure the pumping motion of a hallowed sound,
measure the sanctity of a meaningful swallow,
measure the soft touch of your soul touching mine
 and others'.

Inside a gift package,
inside a passing year,
inside an ever-expanding glee's
a special rose.

Think of a Butterfly

Think of a butterfly's
transparent look,
remarkable hushed ways,
dazzling intent.
Happiness and honor and peace
flow out of your being—
you're in harmony with a butterfly
and don't know why,
yet and still,
you don't mind.
Its charm collects your energy
while you are transfixed watching.
Think of a butterfly,
its stillness and motion
seem to be one action
happening at once.
Two beings—
you and the butterfly, comrades.

A Smiling Tear

A smiling tear whispered,
the universe listened.
A perfect heart sequestered all noises,
a crown—formed out of a rainbow—
sprightly sat above her head,
raindrops crystallized.
She clearly saw the abiding stars shielding
a black knight galloping across the night sky.
She knew him
as a polite tinker of hope.
She barely saw his face,
yet he crowned her smiling tear,
lived in her wishes.
His unbridled love redeemed a dream lost.

A New Love Coming

Pure tears softly beautiful
stranded in destiny
strangely free
alone

Stand under a tree
long enough to see
someone's walking
on a cloud

A new day chirps
at you
warmly
invitingly

An Asymmetrical Conversation

She came for my soul,
I needed it more.

In every avenue of my being,
she searched for an opening.

She blew soap bubbles up my nostrils,
poured snake oil on my head.

She lit fire to my heart,
kicked my manly manner.

She fired torpedoes,
split my lips.

She crushed my last thought,
I sailed away in a bloody vessel.

Reflection

She, invigorated by a passion,
wiggled her nose on my nose.
Without asking, without hesitating,
she excitedly dove into my burnt closet,
weaved through the breached spiderweb,
coughed and choked on the flaky black ashes.
Each broken spun web
represented a leap I'd taken,
I had too many hurting bones to run.
The disturbed breathless ashes,
a delusional mess I'd claimed,
crumbled in the absence of salvation.
My sense, to the uttermost confusion,
lay bent out of recognition.
Her nose sniffed and hunted for signs
I once had smartly lived.
But in her pupils, I noticed a young girl's reflection
sitting in a grass of beautiful-looking wild flowers
decorating a surreptitious medieval pond.

She, invigorated by a passion,
wiggled her nose on my nose.
Without asking, without hesitating,
she kissed the dust on my soul.

A Kiss of Love

A day of embellished love, Valentine's Day,
a day to patch a heart, any day,
a day to be at ease, today.
A simple word spun to life
shifts a fragile intent into action—
a gallon reasons of solitude spinning;
two sets of eyes strangely watching.
Let's count our kisses one by one—
one for the pain that never dies,
one for the love replicating itself,
one for the wish claimed by the fairy.
I'll take one and put it in my fish bowl,
watch it swim and grow day by day.
You take the rest and keep them warm in your heart.
A simple word spun to life
rattles the nights, baffles the days, stirs an
    unborn promise.
Let that promise-to-be kiss a simple word,
let it kiss the wish claimed by the fairy.

Forever

Forever in a place without time
forever in a time of love
forever being a rose
forever kissing me

nights never come
mornings always live
in my heart for you
you're my dream forever

forever the sun ablaze
forever the voice I hear
forever the binding twine
forever the perfect leaf

such time as this time
a time without endings
a time not existing
a time forever

forever the day
forever the wind
forever the touch
forever the dream

you're holding me
I'm holding you
in a place without time
forever

Beloved

Let not a matador near your doorsteps,
keep, too, jumping jacks away.
Stay out of the woods,
walk often to the ocean's shore.

For upon the horizon
sits your beloved
beckoning the whirlwind
cease from toiling.

Put a candle in every window,
forget not the attic nor the basement.
Tend the nights,
guard the days.

Feel timeless,
swim, plan,
engage the touch
flowing in the wind.

I come without a sword,
without a notice sent,
without strings and things—
“a visual moment arriving.”

A Benevolent Warrior

God released him
from his duty to self.
Now he flies without wings,
without protection.

He talks to Frida—
the best woman he knows—
who underscores his significance.
Daily she presses him for a poem.

She has decided he's her poet
though mentally battered is he.
She doesn't understand God's
belligerence toward a tadpole.

Frida, a benevolent warrior,
fights to restore dignity and sanity
to a less than pragmatic goof-off.
God is not on her side / neither is he.

She cradles him,
creates a chef-d'oeuvre out of him,
laughs at God,
defies and counteracts a wrong.

On her own, she's a benevolent warrior,
snatches God's crumb for herself,
transforms him into a titan,
calls him great.

Life Happens

being important
being with a love
being what the universe says
being who you are now

engaging this moment
sharing breath
quivering because life happens
rambling to placate propriety

taming the years left
succumbing to lost
dismissing a created thought
forgetting not what the universe says

seeing a love
shivering over a murmur
shuffling in the sand
stumping the light out

being important
being without a smile
being beautiful alone
being a classical song

Which Way's Home

All the paths knee-deep in mud,
stopped by a church for directions—
young people smiled pretty,
old folks dead or gone.

Can you tell me
which way's home,
all the paths barren,
long and narrow,

dark and blue,
almost frozen,
yesterday's tracks
knee-deep in mud.

All the paths a destined course traveled,
strangers met, steps taken.
I don't know which way's—
Can you take me home?

Five Hundred Poems

Five hundred poems
I spent to find you
lots of words I wrote
even more cast away

Here you are
not kissing my tears
loving me not
honoring only what I spent

I spent, I had too
life wasn't right
neither was I
You built a fortress

You knew I would come
I spent, and you spent
much waste spilled
five hundred poems

Joey, the Impossible Dream

"Joey, come down from the cloud,
come and go home with me."
I am the impossible dream,
immeasurable distance away
from what I ought to be.
Since man I am too,
sporadically I splash in the mud.
On dry land in somebody's sleep
forging ahead is a dream
shining in the space of my mind,
beaming as the star's bright,
spinning thru unlimited loops.
I have nowhere to go,
nothing else to be,
I am the impossible dream,
beholden to what I am—
uncontained by women or beasts—
ether's gravity pulls me away.
Can I for an instance in time

breathe my immortal fate?
Always I am the impossible dream,
immeasurable distance away
from what I ought to be.

Ride to Infinity and Keep on Riding

Climb into your honor-driven time capsule,
space, distance, invention collaborate as one force,
creation spills out and greets you—
an exact, everlasting puzzle to satisfy your curiosity.
Ride to infinity and keep on riding,
zoom away from a corked bottle's existence,
expand self-actuality to the limit,
enlighten the silent nights.
Go somewhere out there for meaning's sake,
pamper your extended, external body.
Ride to infinity and keep on riding,
destiny is you lengthening.

Purpose

What strings words, thoughts, meanings, destinies
together in a heated instance,
what is the solar force releasing?
What is the brilliancy of a half million specks—
specks of inert energy forming to be,
what is the brightest memory in the sky?
What is a clean speck of dust witnessing
in a clear reverse looking glass,
what is two murmurs against many?
What is a single solitude of matter creating,
what is the hope of now,
what is tomorrow's promise?

Surreal

Mother

Mother, now you can talk to me,
did we have it wrong?
You left here peacefully puzzled,
God was tight-lipped as you gallantly died.

Scream

What is this disconnection,
this waywardness?
Fraud?

Crowning a Son

Opening His treasure chest,
invigorating a love,
spilling and manifesting Himself
into His creation.

Little Joe

What are you going to do,
Little Joe, Little Joe?
The day is over,
your night has come.

People are unfamiliar;
your young kinfolks,
your next-door neighbors—
you don't know them either.

On decorative, cracked porches,
childhood schoolmates sit relaxed.
In pretty-old memories,
homerooms teachers are remembered.

Ashes forged out of yesteryears' public lessons
require larger-than-life understanding—
you are not a Muse,
not an accomplished metaphorical fiddler.

What are you going to do,
Little Joe, Little Joe?
Your mother never smiled,
not at her oldest son's ways.

Eyes haltingly sniff at you,
the clouds frostily leak.
Your legacy isn't electrified,
the ground cannot legitimize your life.

An Answer

Every role answers a question,
plays host to God's involved plans.
I am his answer to a scar—
that scar vexing and deceiving an itch.

What about your itch,
that itch you keep on scratching.
Since I am an answer to a scar,
I'm perfectly playing a given role,

destined to act on your behalf.
God's afterthought birthed me into creation—
a patch for cynicism,
a chastened response for a bruising soul.

My role is easy,
I do nothing but think,
then act accordingly,
act for you,

live for you.
I guess I owe you much—
an answer to who you are.
I am your answer.

End of a Legacy

I have slept so long,
eaten so little
so often.
My endearing legacy,
an enduring dream, has ended.

Extend Me

Extend me farther than the plain horizon,
away from this nibbling world,
away from earthy eyes.
Extend me to my sanctuary
where I may lie on top of a moving cloud,
sleep restfully in my own bed.
Extend me, please.

Breeze

silence in the breeze
what's more in thee
spit out thy secrets
why blow thy essence about

doth peace speak without a voice
honoring thy life
as thy shapeless appearance
breezes without a nose

in thee, O breeze
the livings share kinship
rely on the same temperament
running through the universe's veins

'tis not a doubt
the scroll is blank
nothing to say about thee
not a visible vision to see

"search not" you say
"till not the ground
sit still and feel
compassion in me

"come forth my fellow servants
toss aside envy and awe
roam the fields and wade across the oceans
touch the lilies and occupy the sky"

silence in the breeze
silence, silence, silence
"speak not for me with thy tongue
cut it out of thy mouth

"I am far from distress
more than words can announce
I inhabit reality
to be with you"

Ascension

Bedazzled
the fly bedazzled the night
a coronation befitting the heaven happened
it happened to me
the fly that would
the little fly that was
the fly sat on the throne

The Perfect Thought

Gather all thoughts,
blow them out to sea.
As they sail away,
if one shall turn
with tears yet remaining
and stare into your heart,
bow before you unashamedly
with joy and admiration,
it will be the perfect thought.
Speechless though it seems,
that one thought—
greater than a dream—
hears your call,
knows your request,
grants your wishes.
The perfect thought
carries you on its shoulders
to your place of honor,
to your destination.

Remember Me

Play with me,
dine with me,
cuddle my heart's desire.
I give you all of me,
uninhibited emotions,
a heavenly inspired motive for being.

You came to me,
I answered you.
Out of a thousand instances,
your request spun into life.

I am unimportant alone,
not even known;
in you,
I live.

You are a lifesaver—
a temple on an unified hill,
a great possessor of power,
a body of energy,
a lifetime of reflections.

Look into yourself,
see me wandering around.
We are celestial roommates
sharing life together here—
instinctively and creatively.

b

I open myself,
I kiss you—
whoever you are,
wherever you are.

Come heavy man come,
come into my lightness,
release yourself to me.

Stay with me
awhile,
live in my silence.

Give me nothing,
take all I have,
breathe me into your being.

Book me in your lost remembrance,
protect my simplemindedness,
I am a world unto myself unsighted.

Come heavy man come,
you who are dying,
seeking answers as to why.

Ask me for nothing.
Ravage the emptiness
you left behind.

Tell no one about me,
tell them not about my riches,
let them find me on their own.

Hide me, O life, hide me.
Hide me from the spiders that bite,
madly kiss my lips.

I have seen you
shall avoid rest
until you come
sleep in my arms.

I must get out of here
head to a welcoming home
refresher than life-saving water
soother than breaded peace

I sat in the dark,

Poetry is that voice languishing
in a corner alone,
asking you to speak for it.

you noticed me not.

You are breathing into my nostrils.
Are you God?

The author attended The University of Memphis. He left his senior year due to personal tragedies. Later and for a while, he became a public speaker. He has been writing since grade school and has resisted the urge from professional critics wanting him to enter his writings in contests. He has ten purposeful manuscripts and believes it is important that they stand on their own merits. He lives in Memphis, Tennessee, with his two small dogs.

The author wants

you to see him

in his writings.

Printed in the USA
CPSIA information can be obtained
at www.ICGtesting.com
JSHW061227300823
47192JS00027B/339

9 798986 013411